Over the Horizon of Life

By

Chantel Makgoba

Published by
Blessed Thabang Mobosi
Nkomaneni Dan C House No: 0601
Postal Address: PO Box 3275
Tzaneen 0850 Limpopo
South Africa

Email: Blessed.btm@gmail.com
Telephone 072 875 6983
Cell:
061 953 9726 / 067 817 2911

ISBN: 978-0-6399345-8-7

Table of Contents

About the Poet

This is Chantel Makgoba from Rasebalane village. Schooling at Mahlane high School. She is 17 years old. She is an athlete and as well loves javelin   last year (2018) and this year (2019) she got promoted to play in Polokwane for Mopani district. She loves music and music is the only thing that keeps her going, she said. She is a singer. She believes respect is the key to good quality of life. They say you'll never be free if u don't respect an enhance one's freedom. I only see my mother as my inspiration. Why? "Because she faces all things that troubles her without giving up".

I'm only obsessed on getting my people good quality of life not that I have the superpowers to do so but thinking positively can make yourself to see things differently I believe. I believe my calling is to become a Quantity surveyor.

Took me to a way back

It takes a long way back
It reminds me of a way back
If was ticking an I had a ring ball
to complete the tick tock
Eish! I would rather go there and roll like
a roller tape.

I met up with Rollocia
It was like Hell fun!
I wanted to make it Hell fun too!
But on some circumstances
It became sophisticated
All in all

I Salute Africa

New voices from Africa
I wanna move around all mountains of
Africa
Only if I had the voice of mama Africa
A child from Africa
Peace and joy in Africa
Yes of course!

I was born in Africa
I never thought of and sow any continent
beautiful as Africa
Lot of fun in Africa
Precious gift glittering in its pride

There are mountains and values in Africa
The most precious gift God has given to
people of Africa
No starvation in Africa
Might have its own bad, but
It's good in Africa
You only hustle to survive in Africa
Different cultures in Africa
Different believes in African people
But choose wisely

Fortune teller

I wish
I was you
You know what will happen
How come?
How did it happen?
Is there anything you did?
They said no one can predict, but you're
a predictor

I wander how
I wander why
I wander what did you do
What a gift!
It's like a teller scope not just any scope
can be so
You gift doesn't sabotage, but only bring
a smiley face with peace and love you
carry out pure absence with no
complications
With no ramification

No tortuousness to human not
crookedness
You bring knowledge and only guide in
peace

My village

My village
Is a village of Mistry
A village of talents
A village with elegant motions
Glittering in its pride
A village with golden voices
My village for Unity

Feel the millions, see their passion
Their hands are joined together
There is hope in its eyes

Dearest friend

I never got a chance to talk you!
I never got a chance to walk miles with
you. Nothing changed in you from the
first day till now.

You never get to be corrupted
You were standing on the corridors
You never get to be a corrida
How sweet!

You never got into a single combat
Single handed that's what happened in
you

It is really on high rates
When you're called a shepherd
You know how to look after your life, and
people around you, even if they're not
from your family. Every person in your
surroundings you protected them.
With your shawl.

I never sow shameful face on you.
You always smile
I sow the happy face
It is always a happy day to you
Your sentiment was updated

You only treated some of the things in a
sentimentalised manner

Crazy in love

And I never listed to the negative things
they said about love. I was so foolish
Never thought it could come out this way
I welcome you in this darkness world of
mine!

I welcome you in this swarthiness
We have our own differences
You only judged.
You used dark words to my people
In my world.

I never thought it could become dark ages
How little of my mind
Thinking that you would Claw the light
Like the moon light
Like a star in the sky

How could you be so inequity?
How could you be so shabby?
How could you be so ratty?
Your so tatty

So garish
It got to be brassy with you
I never see you barefaced this way
So bald-faced
Yes, bodacious you seem to be
You have an innocent face

but you're insolent
So snotty nosed
I should have listened to my
consciousness.
Now I feel so conservative of you
They say never predict
But I should have seen it coming.

Illness

I ask my self that
Why did he create a human?
Why did God create a person?
Knowing that will get through difficulties

Why now is this illness popular?
Why now people have to face this kind of
difficulty? Ain't we perfect enough an
good enough?

To have this rare disease.
Ain't we are good enough to have the
greatest life with no worries?
Why can't we spend the rest of our lives
with our friends and families with no
disturbance?

Do we have to just let things like this
happen?
But how are we going to over come it

I never got a chance to rest
I never got a chance to harvest what I
have worked so much for.
I only want the best for people around.
My people it's like I'm getting rusted

What a hard worker!

It makes me wander
How pleasant are you before the nation?
Before for your people
You only feel the pleasure before the
nation in large.

We are grateful to have such an
integrated person like you.
Your integrity makes the nation's feel
safe around your presents
Truly you're an intelligent person
In an intelligible way!

All you intend to do is to lead just the
talent in you to explore the allies of your
country an let your loved ones to gain
their trust and hope.

You had to become whoever it is you.
Inspired to be!
Even if it was a bad day
It has to pass, and the sun comes back

It did show that you're interested in your
goals. You listened when they say work
hard and gain lots and when they say
listening is a skill

Lamentation

How lonely is the city?
That was full of people
How like a wisdom is she
Who was great among the greatest in
the nation!

The princess among the royal princesses
has become a slave
A slave in her own life

You get to ask questions
But who will answer?
Only her with the minds
Flashing through her minds
It's so flashiness
To listen to her worries

She weeps bitterly in the night
Her tears are on her cheeks
Among all her lovers
She has no one to comfort her

All her friends have dealt treacherously
with her. They have become her
enemies. Off they are her antagonism

And all her gates are desolater

Her priests resign, her vision is afflicted,
and she is in bitterness

Love potion

You're so magical
Who could have thought of you?
Only to take a sip
I only see magical powers
Love potion
Made me see him differently

How possible Can you be so powerful?
No damage
But you offended my feelings
Cause he never looked me the way I did
What a shame!
A drink credited with power to love
Over love

Love

It's so easy to love
Love flows on the air
More than a bird can fly
You know you can feel love
Appreciate love, adore it, feel for love
But you will never see love
You'll never meet up with love
It's like day light dreaming

The great liking or affection
In love feeling are strong
Stronger that magical powers
Or anything that can be much stronger

You call it crazy in love

You Kept Me Waiting

You kept me waiting
And I kept walking
Trying to find you
Only that I didn't know you turned your
back on my face for good
It's like my life was meant to be so.

You made me smile
 You made me the happiest, I never felt
this way
Your words are so magical
You never gave me the benefit of doubt

You're like a dictionary
You add meanings to my life

So crazy in love

Who could have thought of you?
I'm super blinded by your love
I have been waiting
Yet I saw the love of my heart
It gets to melt when I see you.
Your love is in a sentimental manner

Poetry

Poetry is sort of driven madness
The quality of being rash and foolish
A feeling of intense anger
Obsolescent for legal insanity

Unrestrained excitement or enthusiasm
crazy minded
Fuelled with many thoughts
Intensely enthusiastic
with possessed

inundate excitement bizarre or fantastic
Affected with madness or insanity

Your Current Situation Is Not Your
Destination)
No one is perfect
Nobody has ever had a perfect life
An nobody will
It's only up to us

If we choose to live in a righteous
indignation. Or Choose to live our life's
like nobody's business. Knowing where
we are going.

Don't be ashamed of what has happened
to you, because what has happened to
you has happened for a reason.

The more we deny
The more we abnegate
The more we complain
The more we become complacent
The more we get influenced
We became more influent
And the more we get confused and don't
accept what has happened to us.

Then it doesn't become useful
The moment we start to accept and try to
find what's useful in the struggle.

The things we have been through that's when we will varnish our weaknesses

That's just like us trying to cover all the scars on our faces to look pretty. Turning something that could be ugly into something beautiful and inspiring When what you have been through its inspirational for other people; then it was all worth it. so, don't get stuck on how things used to be.

I once heard a quote that says, "Every next level of your life will demand the new you and sometimes, it takes being broken". In order to become that new version of yourself, just because something is over. It doesn't mean your life is over. Work on your weakest points This chapter is not your story. This moment is not your life. You have to believe the tables of your life will turn.

This pain will become power
This weakness will become strength
This confusion will become peace
Better things are coming for your life.

Your flaw or weakest point can lead to
success. The condition of being
financially weak.

How Could The One Be

How could the one
Who told me that I'm?
Beautiful hurt me so badly?

How could the one
Who told me that I'm precious hurt me so
badly?

How could the one who told me that I
make his days to be phenomenal hurt
my feelings?

You promised to love me and Care for
me
Who told me that we belong together!
You broke my heart!
Where did it go wrong?
What happened to those words you told
me?

Now those words mean nothing to you
I cared for you, now this.
Who will tell me those words except for
you?

Please   dearest
Don't do this to me

Don't pull out your strings on me
Hard to find

Words are everywhere daily
We read them and they fly out
Life is nobody's business
When we are provoked

But there's always something hard to
understand
They are hard to find when they are
needed by heart.

 when the heart feels words hide like
they are not part of life

While words are busy playing some
twisted games
My heart looks sadly through the window
glass, as the raindrops slowly slide down
gently on a bloody lifetime
Hoping that one day
Words will realize what my heart wants
to say.

Real Love

Real love
Doesn't care about body style
Model looks
Or wallet size
It only cares about what's inside

Mistakes never occur
Because it's only the mind that gets
angry, but the heart still cares

Share your thoughts
Show commitment
Show your love
Express your feelings
Be polite
Don't be an Introvert

And what you must know is that
Love always leaves a mark

I Need to Let You Know

I need to let you know
Life is not good without you
Not even perfect
You are my angle

Is like a tap without water
A choir without a conductor
A national without a government

You know how it feels
To be lonely

You are my angle
Come and save me

You really mean a lot
I only look up to you
In terms of need or if in happiness
How great you are
You're so delusional
Only in love

Your reckless in love

You may write me down in history books
With your bitter twisted lies
You may treat me in a dirt way
But still, like dust, I'll rise

Does my sassiness upset you?
Why are you beset with gloom?
Cause I walk like I've got oil walls
pumping in my room

Just like moons end like suns
With the certainty on tides
Just like hopes springing high
Still I rise

Did you see me broken?
Bowled head and lowered eyes
Shoulders filling down like teardrops
Weakened by my soul full Crips

Does my haughtiness afford you?
Don't you take it awful hard?
Cause I laugh like I've got gold miles
Digging in my own backyard

You may shoot me with your words
You may cut me with your eyes
You may kill me with your heartless hand
But still, like eyes I'll rise

Does my sexiness upset you?
Does it come as a surprise?
That I dance like I've got diamonds at the
meeting of my thighs

Out of the hits of history shame
I Rise from a past that rooted in pain

I'm a blaze ocean, leaping and wide
Welling and swelling in bear in the tide
Leaving behind nights terror fear

Into a daybreak that's my ancestor clear
I am the break and the hope of the slave.

You're My Bestie

My headache, my love
My smile, my precious gift
You're like a sea rose

My wrong, my right
My pain, my happiness
My everything
Your mind

I think of you
When I wake up
When I eat, I see you in the plate!
Even when I sleep, I think of you
Your touch
Your voice
You make me to have sleepless nights

I think of you
I just can't talk to you right now
I know that if I talk, I'll regret it late

When you are away
I always think about you
Your smile
The way you talk
It makes me blush

Distance means so little to me
You mean a lot to me
I could walk miles away way until I reach
up to you my destiny

Look in my heart
It is like water in the wall
Love has no boundaries
No limits
It's up to infinity
It can overcome all life.

I love you because you always give me a
reason to smile that always stays on my
face.

www.ingramcontent.com/pod-product-compliance
Lightning Source LLC
Chambersburg PA
CBHW020144150626
46552CB00021B/1661